CARDBOARD ROBOT CHALLENGE!

Sue Gagliardi

T0020300

abdobooks.com

Published by Pop!, a division of ABDO, PO Box 398166, Minneapolis, Minnesota 55439. Copyright © 2021 by POP, LLC. International copyrights reserved in all countries. No part of this book may be reproduced in any form without written permission from the publisher. Pop!™ is a trademark and logo of POP, LLC.

Printed in the United States of America, North Mankato, Minnesota.

052020
092020

Cover Photos: Shutterstock Images, top left, top right, bottom
Interior Photos: Shutterstock Images, 1 (top left), 1 (top right), 1 (bottom), 11, 13, 14, 15, 17, 22 (bottom), 26 (cardboard hand), 28; iStockphoto, 5, 12, 20, 21 (top), 22 (top), 23 (top), 23 (bottom), 26 (hand), 29 (top), 29 (middle), 29 (bottom), 30; JPL-Caltech/NASA, 6; JPL-Caltech/Malin Space Science Systems/NASA, 7; Hank Morgan/Science Source, 8; Louise Murray/Science Source, 9; Kevin Kozicki/Cultura Creative (RF)/Alamy, 18, 31; Barrie Fanton/agefotostock/Alamy, 19; Christina Kennedy/ Alamy, 21 (bottom); Chuck Place/Alamy, 25; Ian Nolan/Cultura Creative (RF)/Alamy, 27

Editor: Meg Gaertner
Series Designer: Jake Slavik

Library of Congress Control Number: 2019955034

Publisher's Cataloging-in-Publication Data

Names: Gagliardi, Sue, author.

Title: Cardboard robot challenge! / by Sue Gagliardi

Description: Minneapolis, Minnesota : POP!, 2021 | Series: Makerspace cardboard challenge! | Includes online resources and index.

Identifiers: ISBN 9781532167935 (lib. bdg.) | ISBN 9781644944530 (pbk.) | ISBN 9781532169038 (ebook)

Subjects: LCSH: Cardboard art--Juvenile literature. | Crafts (Handicrafts)--Juvenile literature. | Creative thinking in children--Juvenile literature. | Maker spaces--Juvenile literature.

Classification: DDC 745.54--dc23

WELCOME TO DiscoverRoo!

Pop open this book and you'll find QR codes loaded with information, so you can learn even more!

Scan this code* and others like it while you read, or visit the website below to make this book pop!

popbooksonline.com/robot-challenge

*Scanning QR codes requires a web-enabled smart device with a QR code reader app and a camera.

TABLE OF CONTENTS

CHAPTER 1
ROBOTS IN THE WORLD

Robots are machines that help people.

People **program** robots to do jobs. The robots then do the jobs on their own.

For example, some robots clean floors.

WATCH A VIDEO HERE!

These robots use high heat to connect parts of new cars.

Others sort through objects. Some

factories use robots to build cars.

The **Curiosity** *robot is about the size of a large car.*

Some places are hard for people to get to. So, they send robots. For example, people have sent robots into space.

ROVERS

Rovers are robots that **explore** places in space. *Curiosity* is one rover. It landed on Mars in 2012. Its job is to find out if life ever existed on Mars. *Curiosity* moves around Mars on wheels. It studies the sand and rocks. It takes pictures with its cameras. Scientists learn about Mars without leaving Earth.

Curiosity *took a selfie on Mars.*

The Dante robot can enter active volcanoes to do science research.

Some places are not safe for people. People can send robots there instead. For example, robots can go

to very hot places. They can even go

inside volcanoes.

Gizmo is small enough to enter collapsed buildings. It helps people with search and rescue missions.

CHAPTER 2
THE SCIENCE OF ROBOTS

People build robots to do certain jobs.

Robots can look very different depending

on their job. But robots have some parts

in common. For example, robots have

LEARN MORE HERE!

Exoskeletons are robots that help people walk. The robots have motors that move the wearers' legs.

plastic or metal bodies. They have motors

and **gears** to help them move.

Each robot has a power source. It might have a battery. Or it might plug into the wall. A robot also has a computer. People **program** the computer. Then the

This robot cuts grass. It runs on a battery.

A computer programmer writes instructions for robots. These instructions are in code.

computer tells the robot what job to do.

And it tells the robot how to do the job.

People are making self-driving cars. These cars can sense other cars around them.

Some robots have **sensors**. The sensors give information about the robots' surroundings. For example, a sensor might tell the location of other

objects. Other sensors might **detect**

gases, light, or temperature.

This robot can clean carpets. Its sensors help it move around a room.

CHAPTER 3
ROBOT CHALLENGE

People can build robots to do almost

any job. Challenge yourself to build a

cardboard robot. Decide what job your

robot will do. What parts would your robot

COMPLETE AN ACTIVITY HERE!

need to do that job? Make a plan for your

robot on paper. Then build the robot.

This girl drew a design before building her robot.

THINK ABOUT IT

Why might it be a good idea to plan something on paper before building it?

Many robots **mimic** the human body. Think about how the human body works. Bones form the body's frame. They connect at **joints**. Muscles stretch or shorten to move bones. And tendons

These boys gave their robot arms and legs.

This boy is using a hot-glue gun to connect parts of his robot. Be careful when using a hot-glue gun. Ask an adult for help.

connect muscles to bones. What materials could you use to connect parts of your robot? What materials could you use as the robot's frame?

This robot is attached to a skateboard so it can roll.

Some robots can move. They have wheels or tracks. And some robots can sense their surroundings. How might your robot move? What materials could you use to mimic **sensors**?

This girl used pieces of paper to mimic buttons on her robot.

This boy used old computer parts to mimic sensors.

SUPPLY LIST

paper towel tubes

cardboard boxes

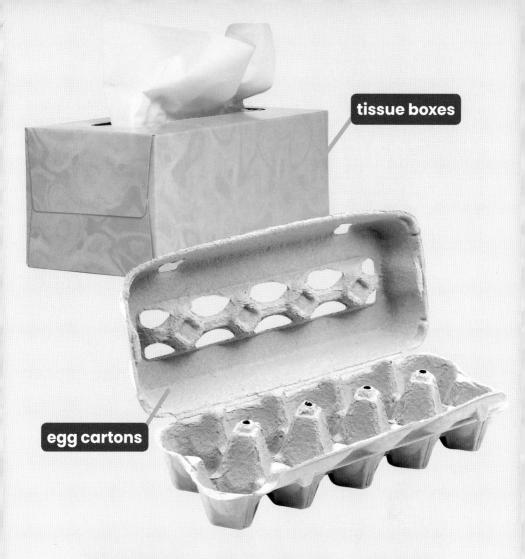

tissue boxes

egg cartons

tape or glue   string or yarn   scissors

paint, markers, or crayons   paper cups

paper fasteners   pushpins

CHAPTER 4
IMPROVING YOUR DESIGN

Engineers often make one form of a robot first. They test the robot. They see what works and what doesn't. Then they make a new form of the robot. They make the design better. You can test your robot too.

LEARN MORE HERE!

Tape attaches the different parts of this cardboard robot.

What do you like about your robot? What

do you want to change?

Consider other designs for your robot.

Many robots **mimic** the human hand.

Human hands can open and close.

Human hands can move in complicated ways.

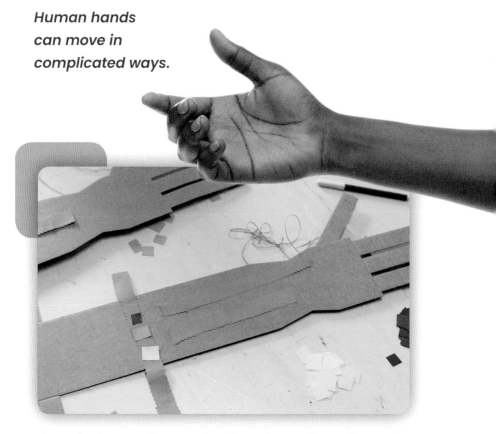

One design makes a robot hand out of cardboard.

Similarly, some robots can grip and pick up objects. How could you design your robot to pick up objects?

THINK ABOUT IT

Why might people design robots to move like humans?

This robot's hands are made of paper.

Another popular type of robot is the robotic arm. It has several parts connected by **joints**. Robotic arms use levers to work. Levers are simple machines. In a lever, a bar moves over a fixed point. The fixed point is called the fulcrum. There are many kinds of levers. They all involve a load, or something being moved. They also involve effort, or work. How could you use levers to build a robotic arm?

People program robotic arms to do the same movement again and again.

TYPES OF LEVERS

FIRST-CLASS LEVERS

Place a load on one end of the bar. Push down on the other end. The load will lift. A seesaw is an example.

SECOND-CLASS LEVERS

Place a load in the middle of the bar. Lift the bar on one end. The load will lift too. A wheelbarrow is an example.

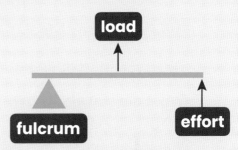

THIRD-CLASS LEVERS

Place a load on one end of the bar. Lift from the middle of the bar. The load will lift too. Your arm is an example. Your shoulder is the fulcrum. Your arm muscles work to raise your hand.

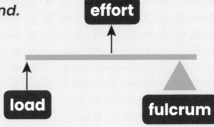

MAKING CONNECTIONS

TEXT-TO-SELF

Have you ever seen a real robot? What was the robot programmed to do?

TEXT-TO-TEXT

Have you read other books about robots? What did you learn?

TEXT-TO-WORLD

This book mentions many jobs robots do in the real world. What are five other jobs robots could do to help people?

GLOSSARY

detect – to find or notice something, especially something hidden.

explore – to move through an unfamiliar place in order to learn about it.

gear – one of many wheels that fit together to help a machine move.

joint – a point where two parts of a structure connect.

mimic – to copy how something looks or acts.

program – to give a computer instructions.

sensor – a device that learns about its setting and sends that information to a computer.

INDEX

ONLINE RESOURCES
popbooksonline.com

Scan this code* and others like it while you read, or visit the website below to make this book pop!

popbooksonline.com/robot-challenge

*Scanning QR codes requires a web-enabled smart device with a QR code reader app and a camera.